The Mystery of the Cliff Houses

By Anne Davies

Contents

The Lost Cows

One cold winter day in 1888, two cowboys rode across Mesa Verde in search of some lost cows. Richard Wetherill and Charlie Mason looked ahead and then out across Cliff Canyon. Suddenly Richard gasped.

There, tucked into the cliff's wall, stood perhaps a hundred golden-colored buildings. "It looks like a palace!" said Charlie.

They decided to cross the canyon and explore.

Exploring the Ruins

It was a hard climb down the canyon wall and then up to the ruins. But it was worth it.

Richard and Charlie found themselves in a silent stone city. They stepped through small doorways into room after room after room. Hundreds of people must have lived here once, they thought.

There was dust everywhere. Some walls were broken down. But beneath the fallen stones and the dirt, Richard and Charlie found painted pots, a stone axe, and, after a bit of digging, three skeletons.

Richard and Charlie named the ruins Cliff Palace.

That night they talked for hours by their campfire. Who had built these ancient homes? they wondered. Why were the homes built in the cliff? And what had happened to the people who had lived here?

Richard wanted to know more. He returned to the ruins again and again to search for clues.

Richard (right) worked in the ruins with his brother John.

Chief Acowitz (left), a leader of the Ute tribe in 1888, and his wife

Richard and Charlie may have been the first people to visit the ruins for hundreds of years. But they were not the first to see them. The Ute Indians, who lived nearby, knew of the abandoned city. But they chose not to visit it. They believed the ruins were sacred and should not be disturbed.

Searching for Clues

It wasn't long before museums in Denver, Chicago, and New York learned about the cliff houses. They sent archaeologists *(ahr kee AHL uh jists),* people who had been trained to study ancient ruins, to work with Richard.

They searched through crumbling rooms. They pushed aside fallen rocks. They dug down deep to find what had been left behind. When the sun set, they worked by the light of lanterns.

Lands of the Ancient People

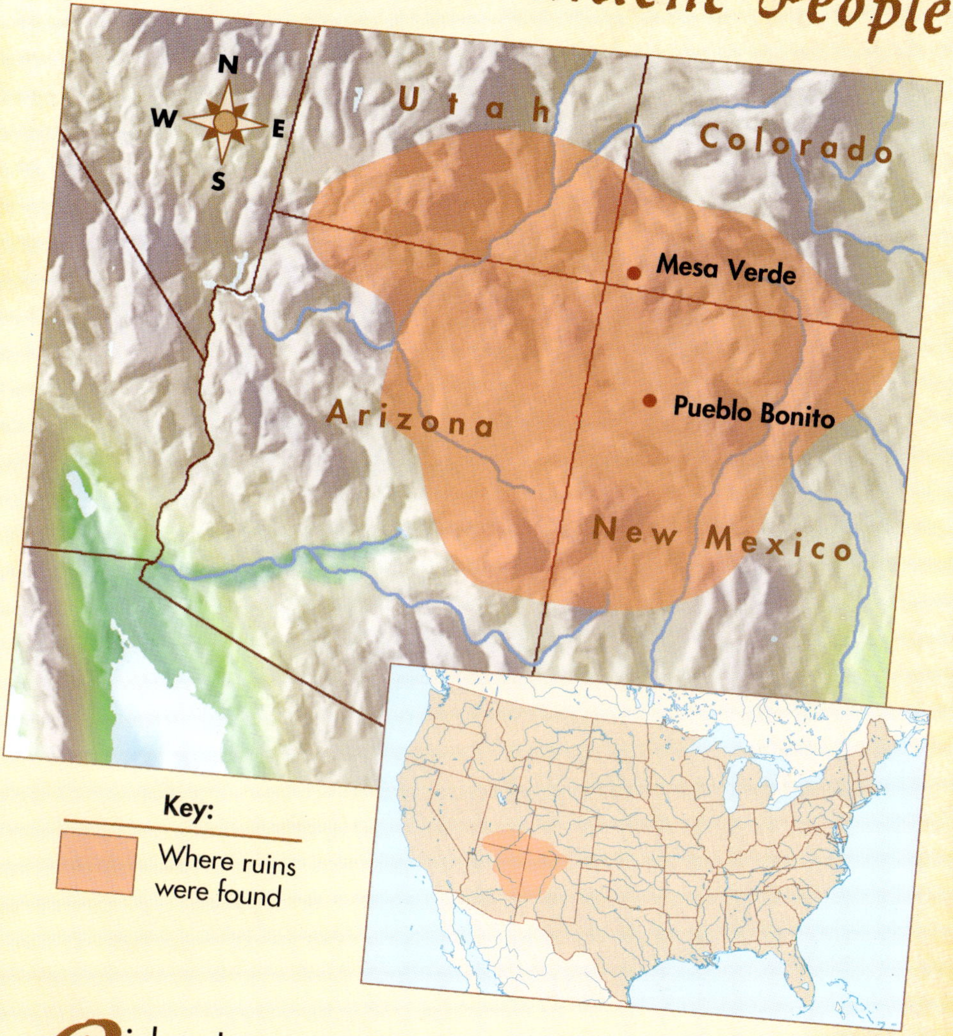

Richard and archaeologists eventually found thousands of ruins across four states: Colorado, Utah, Arizona, and New Mexico.

Crutches

They found countless pieces of pottery in different sizes, shapes, and styles. They found ancient tools. These things were clues that helped show how the people had cooked their food, built their houses, and made their clothes.

A bone needle

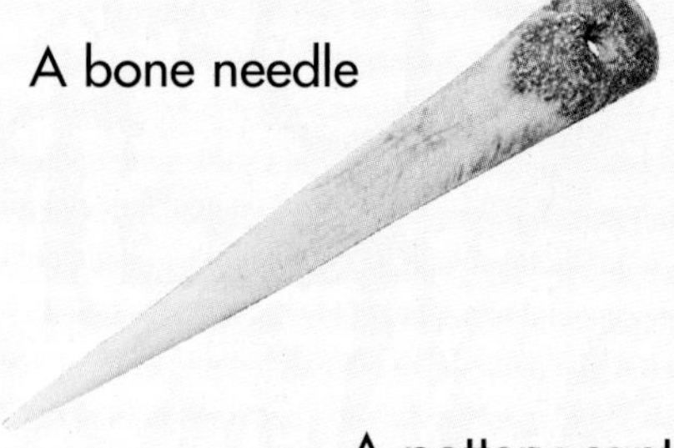

A pottery canteen for carrying water

Not all the ruins they found were built in the cliffs. One of the biggest ruins, Pueblo Bonito, is on a mesa.

One of the best places to look for clues was trash piles! The ancient people threw their trash over the cliffs, behind houses, or in old rooms. Archaeologists found broken pots and broken tools in these trash piles. They also found clues that told them the people ate corn, beans, squash, prairie dog, and antelope.

Beans

Corn

Squash

These stones (far right, bottom) were used for grinding corn.

Sometimes the archaeologists found human graves. Skeletons and mummies showed the ancient people were not tall.

A grown man might have been 5 feet 4 inches tall, about 4 inches shorter than the average modern-day American man. Women were a bit shorter.

In a few places archaeologists found necklaces buried with skeletons. Some were made from seashells from the Pacific Ocean. Since traveling to the ocean took many days, archaeologists think this means the people traded goods with others who lived nearer to the ocean.

Unsolved Mysteries

After studying the ruins for many years, the archaeologists still had questions. What had the ancient people called themselves? They did not leave any writing to tell us. Today, many people call them the Anasazi *(ahn uh SAH zee)*. But the ancient people probably would not have liked this name. It comes from the Navajo *(NAV uh hoh)* language and means "ancient enemies."

Some people prefer to call the ancient people "Ancestral Puebloans."

Why did the Anasazi build so many houses in the cliff? Did they build the houses to be safe from enemies? Or did they build them as shelter from the winter snow and wind?

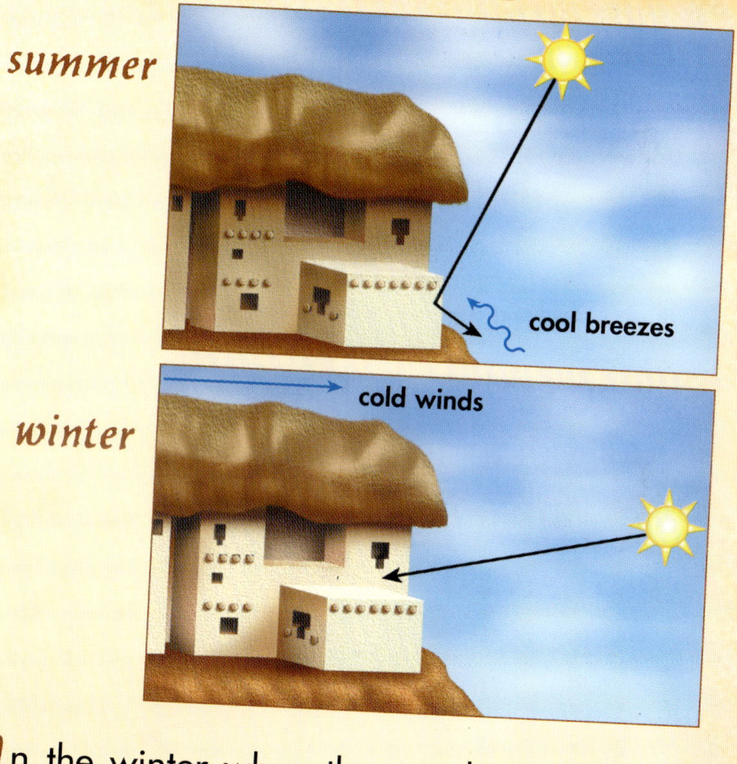

In the winter when the weather on the mesa can be bitter cold, the sun is low in the sky, so it warms the houses. This, along with warm clothes and fire, would have been the only way the Anasazi had to keep warm.

Missing Persons

After carefully studying the cliff houses, archaeologists stumbled on another mystery. They discovered the houses had been built over a period of 150 years. Then no more were built. Why had the Anasazi stopped building houses? Had the people left the cliffs? Had they disappeared?

Did the Anasazi have dangerous enemies? Did they leave when the enemies became too strong? This could be true, but it isn't likely. Tucked into a cavern, the cliff homes would have been easy to defend. And no one has found any signs of ancient battles.

Some people think this tower was built so the Anasazi could watch for danger.

To find out when the houses had been built, the archaeologists looked at wooden beams in the houses. A tree grows a ring for every year that it lives. In warm or wet years, the rings are fat because the tree grows well. In cold or dry years, the rings are thin. The archaeologists compared the rings in the wooden beams with the rings in trees living nearby. They saw where the rings matched. They counted how many more rings the living trees had. This way, they could tell how old each house was.

Perhaps the Anasazi left because they could not grow enough food. Archaeologists know that the last years before the Anasazi left their homes were especially cold and dry. Did it become too cold to live in the cliffs? Was it too hard to grow food and feed everyone?

Archaeologists are still searching for answers. But for now, the story of the Anasazi remains an unsolved mystery.

Archaeologists at work

Index